ISBN 978-0-364-78294-1
PIBN 11270904

English
Français
Deutsche
Italiano
Español
Português

www.forgottenbooks.com

Mythology Photography **Fiction**
Fishing Christianity **Art** Cooking
Essays Buddhism Freemasonry
Medicine **Biology** Music **Ancient**
Egypt Evolution Carpentry Physics
Dance Geology **Mathematics** Fitness
Shakespeare **Folklore** Yoga Marketing
Confidence Immortality Biographies
Poetry **Psychology** Witchcraft
Electronics Chemistry History **Law**
Accounting **Philosophy** Anthropology
Alchemy Drama Quantum Mechanics
Atheism Sexual Health **Ancient History**
Entrepreneurship Languages Sport
Paleontology Needlework Islam
Metaphysics Investment Archaeology
Parenting Statistics Criminology
Motivational

Historic, archived document

Do not assume content reflects current
scientific knowledge, policies, or practices.

SMALL CATCHMENT HYDROLOGY FOR INDIA

KENNETH M. KENT
Chief, Hydrology Branch
Engineering Division
U.S. Soil Conservation Service

Foreign Economic Development Service, U.S. Department of Agriculture
cooperating with U.S. Agency for International Development

ACKNOWLEDGMENT

Great appreciation is expressed for the efforts and expert assistance of Mr. U.S. Madan, Agronomist, USAID, who served as an advisor to the consultant during his stay in India.

Mr. Madan, because of his extensive knowledge of India as a whole and his professional experience, knowledge and genuine interest in India's agriculture and soil and water conservation needs, made it possible for the consultant to obtain much more information from conferences arranged through his assistance with Indian officials at the many government activities and locations visited than would have been possible otherwise.

Small Catchment Hydrology
for India

Introduction

The Government of India (GOI) has indicated a need to improve and
broaden its hydrologic processes for small catchments and improve
hydrologic criteria in order to support adequately the progress being
made in agricultural development programs. Refined hydrologic processes
applicable to all of India should result in reduced costs along with
better performance of conservation measures essential to India's erosion
and water control programs.

Improved hydrologic criteria is needed for (1) the design of water
harvesting programs and facilities for improved efficiency in water
utilization, and (2) refining water balance studies and the overall in-
ventory of surface and ground water resources for agricultural use.
Accepted and approved hydrologic procedures for all of India need to be
available to government officials down through the district level, and to
others who are vitally concerned with and responsible for (1) the improve-
ment and economic design of tanks for domestic use and irrigation, (2) the
determination of the rate and volume of excess water removal needed to design drainage systems for a more economic level of protection, (3) the
establishment of effective and least costly erosion control and water
management practices and (4) the planning of structural systems that are
economically justified for protection from flood and sediment damages in
small catchments.

Suggested Course of Action

In order for applied hydrology to meet a desired level of standards
in small catchments over all of India, procedures and practical guide-
lines should be established and compiled in a handbook for wide distribution. The goal for Donald Vandersypen's USDA/AID two-year tour in India,
which is just beginning, should be to assist the Soil Conservation Branch,
Ministry of Food and Agriculture (MFA), to prepare a "small catchment
hydrology handbook" that will be simple enough for district level technicians to use to properly design soil and water conservation measures.

To successfully complete a handbook for small catchment hydrology
within the two-year period, it will be essential that the MFA (1) promptly
assign a counterpart for the USAID Advisor, eight percent of Mr. Vandersypen's tour having at the time of this report been completed, and to
maintain the same individual in this position for the remaining portion of
the two-year period, (2) arrange for the timely cooperation of other
agencies, especially the Indian Meteorological Department, the Central
Water and Power Comission (CWPC) and the Indian Council of Agricultural

Research (ICAR) to provide existing physical data as it may be needed, (3) provide the services of a limited number of technicians to collect and tabulate raw data for analysis as required, (4) provide the use of computer facilities for expediting some of the analyses, and (5) provide other logistic support necessary for the Advisor and his counterpart to complete progressive phases of the handbook development without delay.

The handbook, developed within the limited two-year period and based on data now available, should be prepared in a manner to permit immediate field applications of the procedures. However, the procedures should continue to be updated to improve the usefulness of the handbook as research results of additional collected data become available.

In order to insure that future data acquisition is most suitable for updating and refining the procedures developed for the handbook, Mr. Vandersypen and the Sedimentation advisors and their Indian counterparts should assist in (1) inventorying the present extent of data acquisition, (2) recommending the type and location of additional data needed, and (3) recommending improved standards for the collection of runoff and sediment measurements.

Indian personnel should be able to continue upgrading the handbook through the training and experience gained during the period of the USAID Advisor's assignment.

Technical Considerations and Findings

This report is based on observations and interviews with personnel at places visited in India between 17 August and 16 September 1970. An itinerary and list of officials visited are included at the end of the report. It should provide guidance for the preparation of a hydrology handbook for small catchments in India. Time did not permit an exhaustive examination of all the resource regions of India but the north-south cross section provided an insight into the range of hydrologic conditions to be dealt with.

It is hoped that Mr. Vandersypen and his Indian counterpart will find it useful during their two-year study and preparation of the hydrology handbook. The completed handbook will contain procedures for use at the District level or lower to estimate the rate and volume of runoff with a reasonable degree of accuracy for any small catchment in India. The size of catchments to which the procedure should apply may range from less than one hectare to about 100,000 hectares. The hydrology for a larger catchment may be obtained by linking together or combining the small catchments which are contained within it.

1andbook will contain procedures for estimating the rate of
sed on individual storms of one day duration or less. The storm
will be for the maximum annual occurrence for various
s. Procedures will be included for estimating volume of runoff
daily and seasonal rainfall and for various frequencies of
э.

volume of runoff for intense one-day storms in a small catchment
a function of the depth of rainfall which may occur over the
and the characteristics of its soil, land use and treatment.

$$Q_t = f(P_t, S, I_a)$$

Q_t = depth of runoff over the catchment during
selected time period (t)

P_t = depth of rainfall over the catchment during a
time period (t)

S = potential maximum retention of water by the soil
in equivalent depth over the catchment.

I_a = initial abstraction including surface storage,
interception by vegetation and infiltration during the period between beginning of rainfall
(P_t) and runoff (Q_t) in equivalent depth over
the catchment.

ate of runoff (q) is a function of depth of runoff (Q_t) for the
se period of storm (P_t) equivalent to the time-of-concentration
tchment and the contributing area. The time-of-concentration
es to the slopes in the catchment, its shape and its size.

$$q = f\left(Q_t, a, \frac{1}{Tc}\right)$$

q = rate of runoff

Q_t = volume of runoff for period t

a = contributing area

T_c = time of concentration

ınual volume of water which a catchment may yield, may be made
ıce runoff (direct runoff), sub-surface runoff and groundwater.
r of the catchment and the evapotranspiration in the area will
ıt considerations for estimating yield in addition to the soil

characteristics and the other parameters that are a function of direct runoff from one day storms. Geology is important to estimating yield in catchments where the intake and deep percolation rates are high. This is usually evidenced by sustained periods of stream flow after storm rainfall has ceased.

Runoff measurements have been made in small catchments at the Soil Conservation Research, Demonstration and Training Centers (SCRD&T) of India. On-site rainfall measurements are being made in conjunction with the runoff measurements. Although most of the records are for periods of 10 years or less they should be quite valuable for testing coefficients and parameters in the procedures that are considered for the handbook. There are many automatic recording stream gages installed on major streams in India; mostly, however with drainage areas larger than a thousand square kilometers. This data, which is on catchments too large to be directly applicable to the handbook procedures, may be valuable for correlating seasonal yield with those derived by the empirical processes in some regional areas. The gaged data for the larger drainage areas may be used to estimate annual yield volumes for the small catchments in the same basin if no appreciable amount of transmission loss or gain takes place between the upper end of the basin and the major downstream gaging point.

There are 350 automatic recording rain gages that have been in operation from 3 to 30 years. Only a few stations have from 20 to 30 years record, 200 stations have records of 10-years or more and the remaining 150 stations have been installed for less than three years. There are 4000 non-recording gages that have been in operation since 1900.

Mr. K.N. Rao, Deputy Director General, Meteorological Department at Poona, and Mr. Ayyar, Hydrologist, Meteorological Department in New Delhi, report that maps showing expected storm rainfall for 1-hour duration and 2-, 10-, 25-, and 50-year frequencies have been completed for all of India. Maps for the 2-, 3-, 6-, and 12-hour durations should be completed for the same frequencies in the near future. The 24-hour, 100-year storm depths are also defined on a national map. The hourly duration-frequency analyses were derived from records for about a hundred recording stations. Most of the station records are for periods of 19 to 30 years. The 24-hour (daily) frequency analysis was made from 4000 gages with records of 70-years or longer.

Visits with Dr. S.V. Govindarajan, Chief Soil Survey Officer, Indian Agricultural Research Institute, and Dr. R.S. Murthy, Southern Region Soils Correlator, established that a major start has been made in soils mapping. Methods being used to classify the soils into a named series are quite similar to those being used in the United States under the direction of Dr. Charles E. Kellogg, Deputy Administrator for Soils, Soil Conservation Service. This being the case it would seem logical that the Indian hydrologic procedures could employ the same four hydrologic groupings of soils as used in the United States. The groupings of soils into four hydrologic groups (A,B,C and D) has proven very useful and quite adequate for the support of small catchment hydrology based on about 15 years of experience in the United States. Dr. Murthy believes that there may be a good chance that a hydrologic grouping can be worked out for key soils series that have been mapped in the southern region of India. These might then be used as a benchmark series for dividing the balance of about 400 correlated soils in the southern region tentatively into one of the four hydrologic groups. The four groupings would include soils that range from those with a very high infiltration rate on the one end to those that are quite impervious on the other.

Our trip to the Bellary SCRD&T center and Regional Pilot Project for Soil and Water Management and our discussions with the respective staffs proved quite enlightening as well as very interesting. We had an opportunity to see and hear about the various characteristics of the black and red soils of this region.

Red soils are usually quite shallow and quite pervious. They present little or no problems from the standpoint of erosion because of their high infiltration rates. The black soils are quite impervious, being made up of a high percent of clay and present a special problem in estimating rates and volumes of runoff. They range in depth from less than 12 inches to over 3 feet. They characteristically develop large cracks during the dry period and close by swelling when the monsoon occurs. However, cracks begin to open again soon after the soil moisture drops slightly below field capacity. This antecedent condition of the soil and its moisture content will greatly affect the amount of rainfall that can be taken in by the black soils. The initial period of rain will be absorbed immediately into the cracks. After enough rain has fallen to cause the cracks to close, the intake rate will be extremely low and the runoff will constitute a very high percent of the remaining rainfall. Many characteristics of the black soils and their variation from one location to another were discussed. It was pointed out that the erosion rates and sediment production rates may be quite different at various locations. However, it appears at this time that the hydrologic characteristics are not too different for the various locations. The soil depth should be a greater factor affecting runoff than any of the other black soil characteristic differences. Although the fertility of these soils is quite high and their production potential good, they are a problem due to their high erosive characteristics.

The hydrologic characteristics of these soils will be more pronounced in the methods for estimating water yield than they will for estimating rates of runoff. Mr. J.R. Coover, ex-USAID Soil Scientist, has reported that, based on his experience, most of the black soils of India would be classified as "D" according to the U.S. hydrologic grouping and that transitional black soils that are more grey in color might belong to the "C" group. Mr. Kester and his Indian counterpart, as well as the staff of the Bellary SCRD&T center, can be of great assistance to the hydrologists in grouping these soils hydrologically since they are being fairly well studied.

Our trip to the Dehra Dun and Chandigarh SCRD&T centers, the tour over the Patiala Pilot Project for Soil and Water Management and discussions with Dr. Suba Rao and his staff at the Forest Research Institute in Dehra Dun provided much insight into the conservation needs and hydrologic problems in northern India.

The SCRD&T centers and the Forest Research Institute are both measuring runoff from forest and hill soils in the foothills of the outer Himalaya mountains. The Patiala project is working on irrigation and drainage problems associated mainly with the Gangetic and Indus Plains. The areas observed are typical of a 1000 kilometer belt along the Himalaya front. The soils of the alluvium in these plains will span the entire range of hydrologic groupings, from sand dunes with the highest intake rate to those with poor drainage and high water tables with very little additional moisture retention capacity. The forest and hill soils appear to belong somewhere in the middle of the hydrologic grouping.

Hydrologic procedures in the alluvial plains must include those for estimating the removal rate and volume of excess rainfall and runoff for an adequate drainage system. The hydrologic need in the forest and hill soils region appears to be the estimation of runoff rates for designing erosion control measures. Here, the land use and its vegetative cover are important variables in determining the potential moisture retention capacity (S) of these soils as contrasted with the high response from the initial abstraction potential (I_a) above the average high water table in the Gangetic and Indus alluvium.

Observations from the plane to and from Poona and Bangalore and our trips by automobile from Bangalore to Bellary and from New Delhi to Dehra Dun, Patiala and Chandigarh show that bunding is a universal practice in India. Bunding stores or detains a certain amount of surface runoff which would otherwise appear at a lower point in the catchment. If the bunding were located on the contour or along a very low gradient it would have about the same effect on runoff as level and gradient terraces respectively. Bunding with closed ends like level terrace, may cause the area to be non-contributing. This would hold true to the extent which the capacity behind the bunding relates to the volume of runoff for a given storm frequency, unless breaching occur.

Paddy fields are another form of land treatment which will need special consideration. The extent to which they will affect runoff will depend on the percent of the catchment area occupied by paddy fields and the dimensions of the ridges forming them.

Conclusions and Recommendations

The following conclusions and recommendations are based on a wealth of data so generously furnished through interviews with the Indian officials and professional personnel listed under the itinerary and acknowledgments at the end of this report. They are derived also from close collaboration with my colleague, Mr. Vandersypen, and are not without the advice of Mr. John T. Phelan and members of the USAID Soil and Water Management staff and their Indian counterparts. Being able to see the major land forms and the physical makeup of much of India, both from the air and at close view on the ground in traveling between the northern and southern regions, contributed to the formulation of the following conclusions. It is somewhat unfortunate that these recommendations are being firmed up prior to the assignment and without the consideration of the Indian hydrology counterpart to Mr. Vandersypen.

A method for estimating peak discharge is needed to construct adequate spillways for all soil and water conservation measures. If the size of outlet is too small the measure will fail and result in property and crop damage in addition to its cost of repair. If the size of the outlet is made too large, it will result in poor functioning of some measures as well as an unnecessary added cost on most measures. Bunding, bench terraces and gradient terraces have a greater potential for reducing erosion and conserving moisture if they have properly designed outlets. These measures and their outlets should be properly sized and installed for many thousands of farms in all parts of India. In order to accomplish this with any rate commensurate with the urgency, all district level technicians, at least, must be able to provide the proper sizing of these measures to the cultivators or to village and block technicians.

(1) There is much hydrologic similarity between India and the United States. It is believed the hydrologic principles that have been successfully applied to small catchments and the soil and water conservation work in the United States should apply equally well to the small catchments and soil and water conservation work in India.

(2) Small catchment hydrology must be derived from rainfall as a major input and combined with the physical characteristics of a catchment. There are hardly any other alternatives since direct measurements of stream flow on small catchments are practically nonexistent. Stream flow measurements are too meager in most countries of the world to provide an adequate basis for operational hydrology in small catchments. It will be many years before enough stream flow data is available to predict the

performance in India's small catchments with their many variations in hydrology.

<u>It is therefore recommended</u> that the hydrology handbook be developed along the rainfall and watershed-characteristic basis.

(3) Procedures should include only those parameters which can be measured, identified or are otherwise available for individual catchments encountered under usual field conditions. For example, the runoff measurements of streams in small catchments are not generally available as noted under (2). Evapotranspiration rates may not be available for some regions in which case they may need to be correlated with temperature or evaporation if one or both are available.

<u>It is recommended</u> the handbook procedures contain only parameters which are workable and applicable for all regions in India and that they be simple enough to be readily computed in the field or presented in charts or graphs from which the desired answers can be quickly read.

(4) There are four major rainfall regions in India:

> (a) Very high annual rainfall, up to 2500 mm. in Assam and along the west coast.

> (b) High annual rainfall, with 1000 to 2500 mm., encompassing a broad belt in the eastern part of the Peninsula merging northward with the northern plains and southward with the eastern coastal plains.

> (c) Moderate annual rainfall, with 250 to 1000 mm. that occupies a belt extending from the Punjab plains across the Vindhya mountains into the western part of the Deccan and widening in the Mysore plateau.

> (d) Low annual rainfall with less than 250 mm. including the Rajasthan desert in the northwest, extending to Kutch and the high Ladakh plateau of Kashmir and thence extending westward to Gilgit.

It is expected that a differentiation in hydrologic procedures for small catchments will need to be made between these four regions. The principal rainfall characteristics that need to be differentiated are (1) the time of monsoon season, (2) individual storm intensities, (3) the persistence or duration of storm occurrences. For this purpose rainstorms or storm occurrences are defined as that rainfall occurring between its beginning and time of cessation. Individual storms would be those separated by one day or longer during which rainfall had ceased.

It is recommended that regional rainfall boundaries be defined on a suitable base map of India and that subdivisions of these regions be delineated if found necessary for any particular hydrologic procedure. For example a further subdivision might be necessary for a procedure estimating the rate of runoff as compared to that necessary for a procedure estimating yield.

(5) A considerable amount of the rainfall data collected in India as described earlier has been analysed for spatial and temporal variations with respect to various frequencies of occurrence. It is believed that the existing analyses will be adequate without any extensive amount of additional data processing.

It is therefore recommended that the extensive list of appropriate publications by Indian authors and a few by authors of other countries, including the U.S., be reviewed to determine the relationship of rainfall intensity with respect to time periods of perhaps 15-, 30-, 60-minute and longer durations for each of the above described regions to determine any need for additional processing of rainfall data. If additional analyses are needed, the processing should be done through an electronic computer in order to keep the development of the handbook on schedule within the 2-year time period.

(6) There are regions in India with soils, climate and land use that are different from those visited by Mr. Vandersypen and myself. Special hydrologic considerations which should be considered in developing the handbook may exist in other regions.

It is recommended that Mr. Vandersypen and his Indian counterpart determine through interview and review of literature the regions in which the application of hydrology for small catchments are enough different so as to require a visit to them to acquire first hand information.

(7) Earlier discussion referred to the paucity of stream gage measurements on small catchments and that gaged data for large catchments could not be successfully used to estimate the rate of runoff on their smaller tributaries. However, a reasonable correlation can often be made between large and small catchments for the 7-, 15-, 30-, and up to 360-day volumes of runoff if the gaged catchments are comparatively free of regulation and diversions; and if there is no large amount of gain or transmission loss in the intervening reaches.

It is recommended that stream gages with daily runoff records for 20-years or longer be examined and a volume-duration-probability (VDP) analyses made for those not regulated.

It is further recommended that the US-SCS computer program be used for the analyses, and if electronic data processing is not available when needed, USATD and GOT should consider makin a a ements to have some of the rocessing done by the SCS in Washington, D.C.

The VDP analyses of data suitable to conditions found in small catchments should be used to test the applicability of handbook procedures for estimating seasonal and annual yield.

(8) The rainfall-runoff measurements and records at the SCRD&T centers visited at Bellary, Dehra Dun and Chandigarh; the Damodar Valley Corporation at Hazaribagh; and the Forest Research Institute at Dehra Dun will provide valuable checks on hydrologic coefficients for various regions and for various catchment characteristics. There are other SCRD&T centers that should have similar measurements. Other agricultural research centers may be collecting some rainfall-runoff data since it is pertinent to many agricultural research objectives.

It is recommended that available reports on all of India's research centers be examined to learn if rainfall-runoff data is being collected and to endeavor to obtain the data.

It is further recommended that the USAID Advisor and his counterpart visit the important locations to become acquainted with the detail of the research centers' work and to obtain the counsel and advice of their local staffs.

(9) Bunding is universally practiced in India. Bunds have been mostly constructed along property and field boundaries that usually do not conform with the topography of the land. Their orientation with the landscape, being inconsistent with the direction which runoff would take, results in a wide degree of hydrologic effects. Runoff will concentrate at the low point of the bunded area and breach the bund if it is not oriented along an approximate contour. Thus, depending on the orientation of field boundaries with the land slope, some bunded areas may breach and contribute to downstream runoff in a slug flow, while other bunded areas may store all of the runoff and remain totally non-contributing to downstream flow.

It is recommended that various classifications of bunding be considered in connection with runoff procedures. One might be in which the bunds are along the contour or along a very low gradient and have an outlet with a relatively low discharge rate. Another would be those that would likely breach from the runoff of nearly every storm. These situations will need to be studied to determine the most practical way in which they should be treated in the runoff equations.

(10) Paddy fields are somewhat similar to bunding in their hydrologic effectiveness. However they are usually flat within their borders. Runoff from individual paddy fields depend on:

(a). The height of the paddy field dikes and their storage capacity to receive and retain rainfall over and above the level of the water supplied by irrigation,

(b) Whether they have provision for drainage when in dry crops or fallow.

It is recommended that special attention be given to orienting hydrology procedures to paddy fields. It will be desirable in deciding upon which hydrologic approach to choose, to consult and work closely with engineers and agriculturists who are studying new ways of managing both bunds and paddy fields.

(11) After studying the hydrologic characteristics of the black (cotton) soils at Bellary, it may be concluded that special emphasis might be given to the initial abstraction (I_a) from runoff. This parameter may be the key to a practical application of hydrologic procedures to this and other similar situations.

The amount of rainfall which disappears into the cracks of the black soils before they swell and close might be quantified by I_a. The coincidence of cracks, antecedent to the design storm, with the most likely date of occurrence would need to be determined in quantifying I_a.

It is recommended that Mr. Vandersypen and his counterpart should, after reviewing various hydrologic procedures heretofore practiced, feel at liberty to explore, with a practical view in mind, new approaches to unique problems. Variations in handbook procedures for various regions should be freely considered.

(12) The triangular hydrograph has proven to be a useful tool in small catchment hydrology. Its geometric shape makes it more easily described mathematically than the conventional curvilinear unit hydrograph. It is simple to work with and can be an adequate presentation of the rate of runoff from individual storm occurrences over a given catchment. The triangular hydrograph can be appropriately used as a unit hydrograph for a given catchment by studying the relationship between time-to-peak (T_p) and time-of-recession (T_r), which are the rising and recession sides of the triangle respectively.

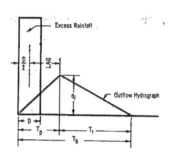

    If a large drainage area is being considered within which two or more small catchments are included, the triangular hydrographs for each can be combined to describe a hydrograph for the larger area. They may be combined by positioning each with respect to their travel time to the outlet of the larger contributing area. This is possible if only a negligible amount of valley or floodplain storage is involved that would otherwise attenuate the peaks and change the T_p and T_r relationships of each. This has proven to be a very useful tool in designing tanks and other storage structures where the size of spillway depends on the amount of temporary and surcharge storage available.

It is recommended that applications of the unit triangular hydrograph be considered for inclusion in the handbook.

    (13) The values assigned to some coefficients in the original edition of the handbook may of necessity need to be somewhat speculative. Some good research and investigation work has been accomplished as was evident at the Bellary, Dehra Dun and Chandigarh SCRD&T center and at the Forest Research Institute at Dehra Dun. Although the handbook procedures may not be expected to change as more research data is acquired, values for their coefficients and parameters should continually be improved. Short term measurements (3 to 5 years) at many well-selected and distributed sites that measure the runoff from unit source areas and under various climatic and land use conditions could greatly strengthen the applicability of the procedures for achieving greater economy in design.

It is recommended therefore that Mr. Vandersypen and his counterpart be invited to participate in ICAR meetings when research on surface runoff and related objectives are being reported and planned.

ion should be given to a review of the work by this
ely six months prior to the completion of the hand-
r. Vandersypen's tour. After having shared some of
r decisions thus made for the beginning of the hand-
hrough some correspondence during the period of
 be beneficial to review and discuss the tentative
r the handbook. The appropriate time for this review
rocedures were drafted by Mr. Vandersypen and his
e any extensive distribution and review of the
tiated.

Chronology of Meetings and Travel by the Consultant [1]

Itinerary

Sunday, August 16

      Arrived in New Delhi.
      Met at the airport by John T. Phelan

Monday, August 17

      Check in. Met with Clarance Gulick, Deputy Directo.
           USAID; Dr. Russell Olson, Assistânt Dir
           AG; Oliver A. Bauman, Deputy Assistant
           Director, AG; and other AID staff.
           Met with Dr. Krantz of Ford Foundation i.
           afternoon.

Tuesday, August 18

      Visited Indian Agricultural Research Institute and ⟩
           Drs. Michael and Arora
           Met Dr. Pois Coddon and other offices of
           Water and Power Commission. Visited th
           and soils laboratory.
           Met J.K. Ganguly in the afternoon.

Wednesday, August 19

      Met with Messrs. Ayyar and Abi of Meteorological De
           D.V. Gulati of CWPC, S.V. Govindarajan o.
           India Soil and Land Use Survey Organiza
           and N. Patnaik of Indian Council of Agr.
           Research Institute.

Thursday, August 20

      New Delhi to Poona via air.
           Met at the airport by B.N. Rakshit and V
           Bannur of Maharashtra Agricultural Depa:

---

[1] See list of persons contacted for details.

<u>Friday, August 21</u>

> Met with K.N. Rao, R.K. Misra, and C.E.J. Daniel of
> Meteorological Department, V.R. Ghangurde of
> Agriculture Department, and R.D. Gupte and V.S.
> Nene of the Water Resources Investigation
> Circle.
> Visited Soil Salinity Laboratory and Soil Survey Office of
> Maharashtra.
> Poona to Bombay in the evening via air.

<u>Saturday, August 22</u>

> Bombay to New Delhi via air.

<u>Monday, August 24</u>

> New Delhi to Bangalore via air.
> Met at the airport by M.P. Cox.

<u>Tuesday, August 25</u>

> Bangalore to Bellary by automobile.
> Met with D.W. Haslem, Gerald Kester and Eugene W. Shaw,
> USAID.

<u>Wednesday, August 26</u>

> At Bellary.
> Visited Soil and Water Management Project.
> Met with M.P. Jahagirdar, and other staff of the project.
> Visited Soil Conservation Research Demonstration and Train-
> ing Center. Met with Balvir Verma and other
> officers of the Center.

<u>Thursday, August 27</u>

> Bellary to Bangalore via automobile.
> Met with Dr. K.S. Murthy, Southern Region Soils Correlator
> and other officers.

<u>Friday, August 28</u>

> Bangalore to New Delhi via air.

Monday, August 31

New Delhi to Dehra Dun via automobile.
Visited Soil Conservation Research, Demonstration and Training Center. Met with K.G. Tejwani, S.K. Gupta
and other officers of the Center.

Tuesday, September 1

At Dehra Dun.
Visited runoff plots at Rajpura and Slip Stabilization work,
accompanied by B.K. Suba Rao and B.G. Dabral of
Forest Research Institute and K.G. Tejwani,
S.K. Gupta and H.N. Mathur of SCRD&T Center.
Met with S.K. Seth, I.M. Qureshi and other officers of
Forest Research Institute and with K.G. Tejwani
and S.K. Gupta of SCRD&T Center in the after-
noon.

Wednesday, September 2

Dehra Dun to Patiala via automobile.
Visited Soil and Water Management Project at Patiala,
accompanied by H.Y. Cott, Howard Ivory and K.E.
Larson of USAID and J.N. Sharma, Kartar Singh,
Gurbachan Singh and Jagir Singh Khera of the
Project staff.

Thursday, September 3

Patiala to Chandigarh via automobile.
Visited Soil Conservation Research and Demonstration Center,
accompanied by E.P. Vance (USAID), G.S. Dhillon,
and I.I. Erasmus.

Friday, September 4

Chandigarh to Srinagar via air.

Saturday, September 5 to September 8

At Srinagar. Attended AID Conference

Wednesday, September 9

Srinagar to New Delhi via air.

Monday, September 14

Met with B.B. Vohra, Dr. N.D. Rege, J.K. Ganguly, and J.S. Bali.

Wednesday, September 16

Left for United States.

Note: Mr. John T. Phelan, Chief, AG/SW, accompanied the consultant to Bangalore and Bellary.

Mr. D.R. Vandersypen toured with the consultant on all field trips.

Mr. U.S. Madan accompanied the consultant to Poona, Bombay, Dehra Dun, Patiala, Chandigarh and Srinagar.

List of Persons Contacted

Central Government, Ministry of Food, Agriculture, Community Development and Cooperation

B.B. Vohra, Joint Secretary
N.D. Rege, Joint Commissioner, Soil Conservation
J.K. Ganguly, Deputy Commissioner, Soil Conservation (Forests)
J.S. Bali, Deputy Commissioner, Soil Conservation (Engineering)

Central Water and Power Commission

I.C. Dos M. Pois Coddou, Director, CSMR Station
D.V. Gulati, Director Surface Hydrology
M. Hedge, Deputy Director, CSMRS
B.M. Gulati, Extra Assistant Director, CSMRS
Tara Singh Sidhu, Extra Assistant Director, CSMRS

Indian Council of Agricultural Research, New Delhi

S.V. Govindarajan, Chief, Soil Survey Officer
N. Patnaik, Assistant Director General, SS and WM

Dehra Dun

K.G. Tejwani, Incharge Soil Conservation Research Demonstration and Training Center

S.K. Gupta, Soil Conservation Officer (Engineering), SCRD&T Center

Chandigarh

I.I. Erasmus, Soil Conservation Officer, Incharge Soil Conservation Research Demonstration and Training Center

Raghu Nath, Research Assistant, SCRD&T Center

Bellary

Balvir Varma, Soil Conservation Officer, Incharge Soil Conserva-

ɾ Delhi - Indian Agricultural Research Institute

I.M. Michael, Associate Professor of Agricultural Engineering
D.R. Arora, Associate Professor of Agricultural Engineering

ιra Dun - Forest Research Institute & Colleges

S.K. Seth, President
I.M. Qureshi, Director, Forest Research
B.K. Suba Rao, Senior Research Officer
B.G. Dabral, Research Officer
B.C. Ramola, Research Assistant

ɾ Delhi - Meteorological Department

P.S. Harihora Ayyar, Meteorologist, Hydrology
S.D.S. Abi, Meteorologist, Hydrology

na - Meteorological Department

K.N. Rao, Deputy Director General
R.K. Misra, Meteorologist
C.E.J. Daniel, Meteorologist

te Maharashtra
oona

.R. Ghangurde, Joint Director, Agriculture (Irrigation)
.D. Gupte, Superintending Engineer, In charge Water Research
Investigation Circle
.S. Nene, Executive Engineer, Design Division, Water Resources
Investigation Circle
.N. Rakshit, Geologist, Groundwater Agriculture Department
.B. Bannur, Deputy Director Agriculture (Irrigation Unit)
.K. Buzruk, Chief Soil Survey Officer, Maharashtra
.G. Dadhe, Soil Correlator, Maharashtra
.B. Mahajan, Agricultural Officer, In charge Soil Salinity Labora-
tory

State of Punjab
 Chandigarh

 G.S. Dhillon, Chief Conservator, Soils

 Patiala

 J.N. Sharma, Deputy Director of Agriculture and Project Officer,
  Regional Pilot Project for Soil and Water Management
 Gurbachan Singh, Agricultural Development Officer (Engineering)
 Kartar Singh, Agricultural Development Officer (Soils)
 Jagir Singh Khera, Development Officer (Agronomy)

Indian Council of Agricultural Research
 Bangalore

 K.S. Murthy, Southern Region Soils Correlator, Institute of
  Agricultural Sciences

State of Mysore
 Bellary

 H. Seshagiri Rao, Agricultural Development Officer (Engineering),
  Regional Pilot Project
 Balvir Verma, Soil Conservation Officer, Soil Conservation Research
  Demonstration and Training Center
 S. Chittaranjan, Assistant Soil Conservation Officer (Engineering),
  Soil Conservation Research Demonstration and Training Center
 N.P. Jahagirdar, Deputy Director, Agriculture and Project Officer,
  Regional Pilot Project for Soil and Water Management
 A.S. Puttu Ram, Agricultural Development Officer (Soils), Regional
  Pilot Project for Soil & Water Management
 M.K. Kulkarni, Agricultural Development Officer (Agronomy),
  Regional Pilot Project for Soil and Water Management
 B.R. Hayavadanachar, Assistant Agricultural Officer, Regional
  Pilot Project for Soil and Water Management

USAID Personnel

New Delhi

Clarence Gulick, Deputy Director, USAID
Russell Olson, Assistant Director, AG
Oliver A. Bauman, Deputy Assistant Director, AG
John T. Phelan, Chief Soil and Water Management Division

Bangalore

Murray R. Cox, Project Leader, Soil and Water Management, Pilot
  Project at Bellary

Bellary

D.W. Haslem, Agricultural Engineer and Team Leader, SW Management
  Pilot Project
Gerald Kester, Soil Scientist, SW Management Pilot Project
E.W. Shaw, Agronomist, SW Management Pilot Project

Chandigarh

E.P. Vance, Project Leader, Soil and Water Management Pilot Project at Patiala

Patiala

H.Y. Cott, Agricultural Engineer and Team Leader, SW Management
  Pilot Project
K.E. Larson, Soil Scientist, SW Management Pilot Project
H.M. Ivory, Agronomist, SW Management Pilot Project

CPSIA information can be obtained
at www.ICGtesting.com
Printed in the USA
LVHW021509261118
598291LV00012B/1207